THE ART TRUCKS OF JAPAN

TRUCKING ART®

Color and sparkle on the highways of Japan

By Clive France

When Momojiro roared onto the screens of Tokyo's movie houses in the 1975 hit *Truck Yaro!*, Japan was on a roll. The economy was booming, the war was a fading memory, and people felt liberated for the first time in decades.

The nation was ready for some color, and the film's swaggering protagonist, played by the striking Bunta Sugawara, captured the spirit of the moment.

Scrappy, tough and outspoken, Momojiro plays hard and works harder, hauling freight across the country in a big rig known affectionately as "Ichibanboshi." And as much as Sugawara's performance, it was this truck and others like it in the movie that launched the series.

From its radiator grill to its trailer rear doors, Ichibanboshi is decorated in banks of colored lights, lengths of aluminum piping, and sheets of shining steel etched with swirling patterns. Down each side is painted a trailer-long flying fish—one is lurching from the ocean, the other is in full flight. Mt. Fuji rises from a distant horizon, and across the trailer's top in bold lettering is Momojiro's personal motto: "A man's journey is alone."

Japanese moviegoers loved it, and a new word was quickly coined—"dekotora" (decorated trucks). Soon after, colorfully decorated trucks began appearing on roads throughout Japan, their presence at night declared with banks of flashing illuminations.

Sightseeing buses, U.S. military vehicles and even ambulances were gutted for their parts. Ignoring legalities, truckers affixed patrol lights to their cabs. Trailers were given stylized paintjobs that often included Edoesque images. Depictions of dragons, fish, mountain landscapes, cherry blossom and characters from kabuki theater caught the national mood. As these vehicles crisscrossed Japan hauling goods, the highways became their catwalks.

Some 30 years on, decorated trucks are still around. Their position in popular culture has slipped, but the passion among enthusiasts remains strong. And no longer do drivers have to strip scrap vehicles for parts to decorate their rigs with.

Today, there is a small industry catering to owners of dekotora. Accessory makers provide everything from Hello Kitty seat covers to illuminated hubcaps. Superstores selling almost solely to the truck crowd can be found on many major highways. Magazines such as *Camion* and *Truck King* keep enthusiasts informed. And skilled body painters are never out of work, as drivers line up to have their artistic ambitions realized across the sides of their vehicles.

Familiar themes include dragons, Heian-era courtesans, flower gardens, and characters from Buddhist mythology and *noh* theater. Christian Lassen-style ocean scenes that invariably feature dolphins under a starlit sky are popular. Pop culture influences are increasingly common, with trucks decked out like shrines to favorite pop singers and anime characters, and even to owners' pets.

These "soft" designs reflect the tastes of the hobbyists that have come to characterize the dekotora world in recent years. Although many are from blue-collar backgrounds, their trucks are mostly pastimes to be enjoyed at weekends. Owners clubs that hold regular meets can be found all over Japan. Families are encouraged to join, and barbecues, party games and amateur photo shoots are the norm. Charity events are held for causes that include police safety, a far cry from the days when truckers and traffic cops were adversaries.

This popularization of dekotora has not been welcomed by all. Some professional drivers view this rush to include all as an affront to the true spirit of dekotora. This has led to a revival in recent years of the simpler designs of the past.

Retro trucks sport "flat" bumpers, illuminated bus signs and large square brake lights. Body art will often depict fish and ocean images that reflect dekotora's links to the ports of Japan's northeast. Trailer rear doors are sometimes decorated with fishermen's prayers spelled out in brush-stroke lettering. There are even faithful reproductions of Ichibanboshi and other trucks from the big screen.

Other drivers have attempted to check this creeping "feminization" with brash designs influenced by mecha anime such as Gundam. These use generous amounts of aluminum and steel piping around the cab and taillights, projecting an image of belligerence that some car drivers find intimidating.

Steel bumpers encrusted with lights jut out snowplow-like, threatening to scoop up anything in front. Canopies of aluminum tubing act as visors that come alive at night with illuminations. Wing mirrors are mounted far in front of the driver on metal arms, and cylindrical aluminum tubes, known as "rockets," thrust out like metallic horns. At the back, elongated exhaust pipe connectors, or "muffler cutters," resemble gun barrels pointed at following vehicles.

With some dekotora costing as much as a small house, it comes as little surprise to find trucks that have been refurbished to offer many of the comforts of home.

Examples abound, such as one large vehicle that has had two sumptuous rooms fitted where crates of goods would once have been stacked. The two areas, separated by a wooden door, boast plush padded walls and soft carpets. Furnishings include the obligatory TV and audio system, an air-conditioner, chandeliers, and a low table with *zabuton* cushions to seat four.

Cab interiors provide ideal canvases for self-expression as well. Many are thematically styled—a traditional Japanese room with *tata-*

mi and sliding doors behind the driver's seat; a spaceship from a '60s sci-fi movie complete with pink and white cockpit seats—while others are shrines dedicated to a singular passion—a pet dog, Hello Kitty, a driver's family, a movie star.

Decorated vehicles are not unique to Japan. In Pakistan and Afghanistan, trucks adorned with Islamic images and swirling arabesque designs are the rule rather than the exception. In the Philippines, Jeepney taxis leave the factory decorated with oversized front bumpers, colored lights and distinctive paintjobs.

But Dekotora are uniquely Japanese. The attention to detail, the blending of new and old, the ease in which technologies are adopted, the wealth of products available, and the willingness of enthusiasts to spend large amounts of money—all are attributes common to the wider Japanese society, where craftsmanship is held in high esteem, leisure time is prized and opportunities for colorful display are few.

Dekotora enthusiasts are said to be a dying breed. The release of this book probably won't slow that decline. However, it is hoped that the stunning photographs that fill these pages will be recognized for what they are—a nod of gratitude to the thousands of nameless drivers that, for the past 30 years, have brought color and sparkle to the highways of Japan.

cocoro books is an imprint of DH Publishing, Inc.
First Published 2008
Text and illustrations ©2008 by DH Publishing, Inc.
ISBN: 978-1-932897-43-2

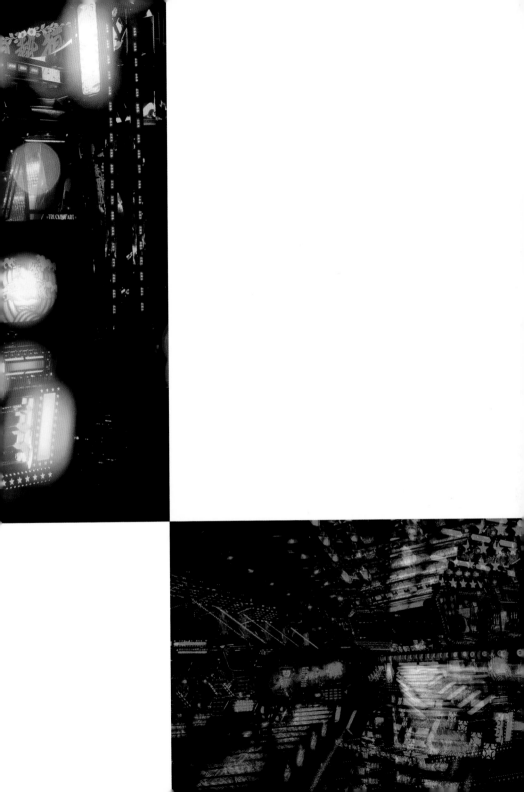

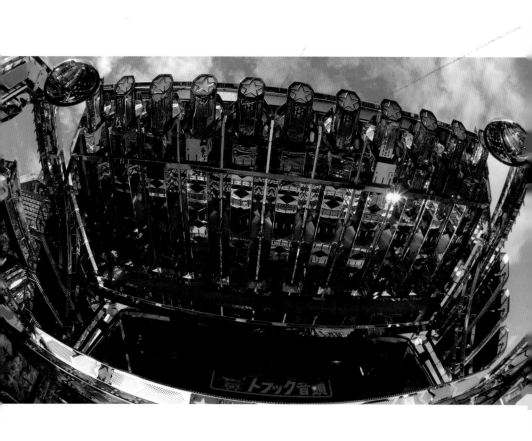

18

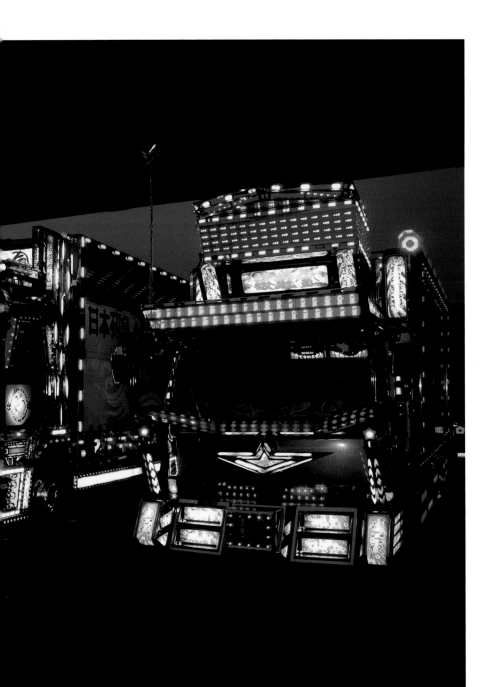

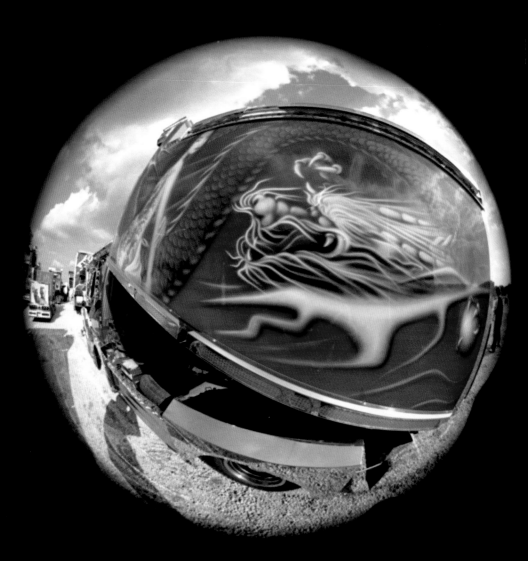

47

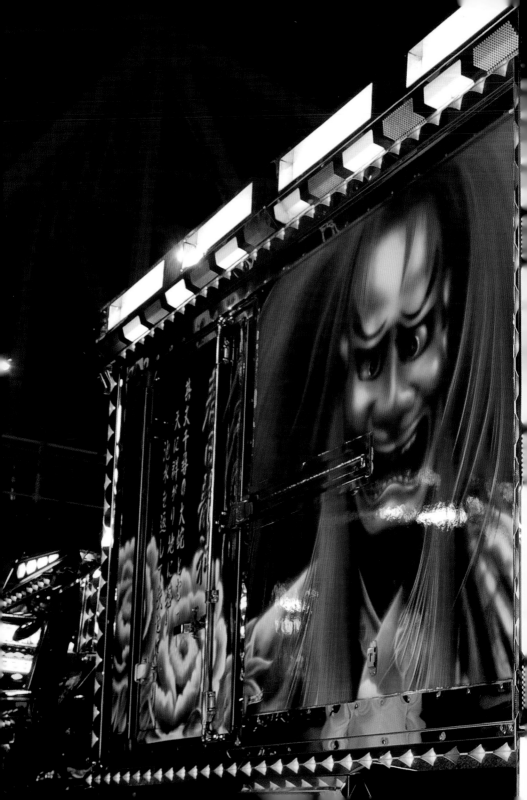

73

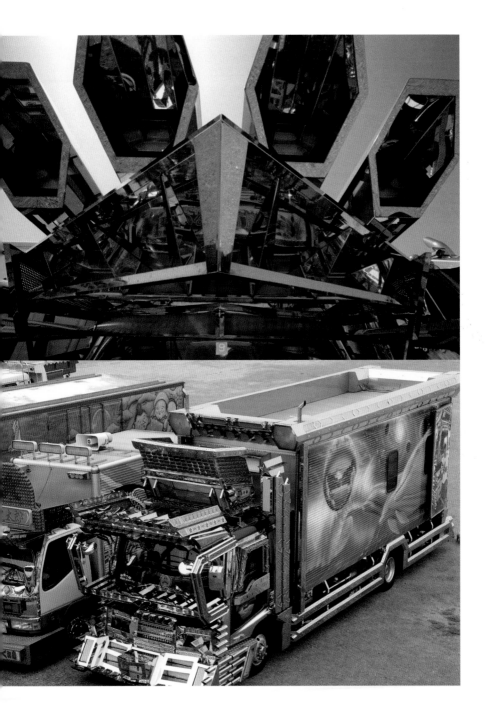